HONOR GIRL

Maggie Thrash

CANDLEWICK PRESS

2

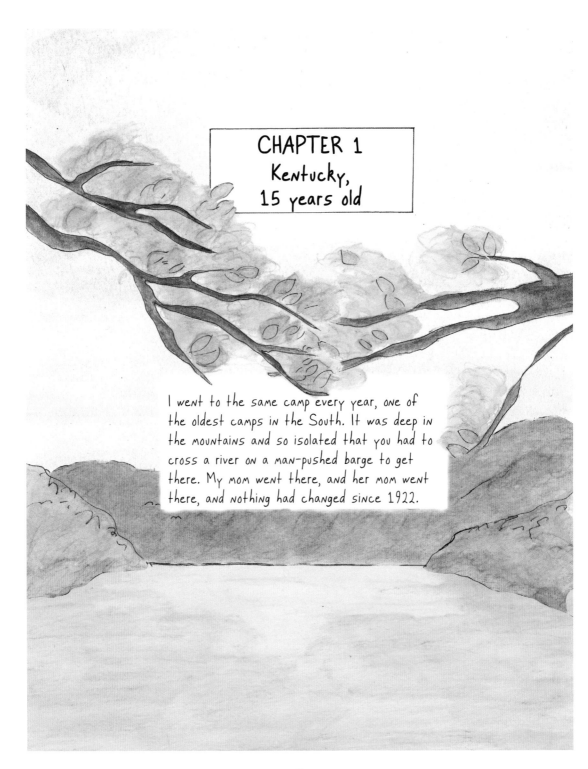

CHAPTER 1
Kentucky,
15 years old

I went to the same camp every year, one of the oldest camps in the South. It was deep in the mountains and so isolated that you had to cross a river on a man-pushed barge to get there. My mom went there, and her mom went there, and nothing had changed since 1922.

There were mandatory Civil War reenactments every morning.

It was literally the blues screaming "blue" and the grays screaming "gray" for twenty minutes.

I had a pillow with all my merit patches sewn on it.

I also had a leash I was supposed to wear at night to prevent sleepwalking, a problem I'd had since I was five.

Everyone had to wear a uniform. My school had a uniform too, so I was used to it. I was used to environments where it was important for everyone to be the same.

There was very little diversity among the one hundred campers. Even the one Jewish girl had blond hair and blue eyes. Her name was Lexi, and every year she set the trends, like what to put in your hair and the right kind of socks and rolling the waistband of your shorts to make them shorter.

CAMP BELLFLOWER

GREENBRIAR MOU

APPALACHIAN

RIVER

Most of the other girls were from Kentucky. They lived in the same towns as one another or went to the same boarding schools. I was the only girl from Atlanta.

OZARKS

MISS

ATLANTA

Which meant I could be a completely different person if I wanted to.

M. THRASH

This was Erin.

SORRY!

THOSE POOR CHILDREN.

COME ON, LET'S GO TO DINNER.

I knew Erin, but only because the same girls came to camp every year. I knew she was 19 and that she played guitar.

I don't think she knew anything about me.

HEY MAG, DID Y'ALL TAKE THE SEX POLL?

WHO'S KEVIN? KEVIN BACON?

NO.

KEVIN RICHARDSON.

OOOKAY.

Kevin Richardson was my favorite Backstreet Boy. I loved him because he seemed soulful and brooding, and he wore dark, billowing trench coats. You couldn't find boys like that in the South. At least not in my school.

Our camp director was an old man who came out occasionally to threaten us with a canoe paddle.

He was ancient and couldn't tell any of us apart. If you ever got in trouble, he'd probably call the wrong set of parents. But that was a moot point anyway, because no one ever broke the rules.

HAVE A NICE SUMMER, GLADYS.

OKEY-DOKE.

There was a 50-cent Coke machine behind the canoeing shed, strictly for counselors. Everyone knew it was there, and every day presented a hundred opportunities to slip behind the shed and sneak a wonderful, refreshing can of Coke. But I never knew a single girl who ever did, including me. That's just not who we were.

Who we were was a bunch of Christian girls who sang songs together. On the first night, we always serenaded the Honor Girl, a 16-year-old camper appointed the previous summer. The criteria for Honor Girl were vague, with no particular definition. It was just the one who seemed, in an unmistakable way, to represent the best of us. Everyone would light a candle, and at the end of the song, we'd each touch our flame to hers. It was meant to be symbolic — the Honor Girl imbuing us with her perfect spirit.

TAPS ALREADY?

WE HAVEN'T BRUSHED OUR TEETH YET!

GO AHEAD. JUST BE BACK IN FIVE MINUTES.

MAKE SURE MAGGIE KEEPS HER LEASH ON. SHE'S SO BAD!

I'LL WATCH HER. NOW, BE QUICK!

SO.

WAIT, WHAT AM I DOING HERE?

OH, YEAH! I CAME TO GIVE YOU THIS.

MY CAMPERS MADE IT FOR YOU.

. . . GOSH.

WAIT, AM I . . . A PSYCHOTIC BIRTHDAY GIRL?

I THINK IT'S A WITCH'S HAT. THEY FORGOT TO DRAW THE BRIM.

AH, OF COURSE.

SO, SLEEPWALKING . . . THAT'S SO COOL.

IS IT?

I ALWAYS BUMP INTO STUFF AND WAKE EVERYONE UP.

IT'S DEFINITELY COOL.

IT'S LIKE . . . THE NIGHT IS CALLING TO YOUR SPIRIT.

BUT . . .

IT'S PROBABLY SAFER NOT TO ANSWER.

HEY, CHICKADEES.

HI, MARY KELLY.

JILL'S LOOKING FOR YOU. I THINK SHE WANTS TO BE YOUR CANOEING PARTNER.

OH GOD.

MAAAAAGGIEE!

LET'S FUCKING ROW!

CHRIST, JILL. AREN'T YOU LIKE TEN YEARS OLD?

Every year I did canoeing because my mom did canoeing and her mom did canoeing. The boats were divvied up by height, and I was too short to row with anyone my own age. It never used to bother me, but now suddenly it really did.

ACTUALLY I'M NOT DOING CANOEING THIS YEAR.

WHAT?

The rifle range was the highest point in camp. It was such a hike that plenty of girls never even went there. That's part of why I liked it. I also liked the smell of gun smoke and bore solvent, and the hundred years' worth of brass bullet shells covering the ground. And the way the crack of every shot echoed down the hill.

WHAT ARE YOU DOING HERE?

This was Libby, the top shooter in camp.

JUST . . . SHOOTING, SAME AS YOU.

OH, OK . . .

WELL, I JUST . . .

I GUESS I THOUGHT I HAD THE RANGE TO MYSELF.

WELL, NOW WE HAVE IT TO OURSELVES.

. . . GREAT.

Libby and I were both shooting for our Distinguished Expert certification, the highest award offered by the National Rifle Association. She was way better than me and had only 10 targets left. I had 33.

LIBBY, EXCELLENT.

MAGGIE . . . I THINK YOU MISSED THE TARGET.

Nicky, head of rifle

LIBBY!

HEY GUYS!

NICKY, I'LL BE RIGHT BACK.

SURE.

SERIOUSLY, MAGGIE, DID YOU EVEN AIM?

I THOUGHT I AIMED. . . .

SUP, SHOOTER.

Whenever it rained, we were immediately herded to the play hall, where the counselors would come up with some extravaganza to keep us from getting depressed. Usually it was a variant on the talent show, with a theme like Memorable TV Commercials or Disco-Rama: Hits of the '70s.

O-Town was the lamest boy band in the history of boy bands. Their only hit was called "My Liquid Dreams," and it was the stupidest song ever. Not a single member of O-Town approached the hotness or soulfulness of Kevin Richardson.

Tennis Bethany wasn't someone I'd hung out with before. She was younger than me, 14, and the different age groups didn't mix too much. I knew she was a National Junior tennis champion, and that she went to a weird Quaker school where all the teachers were hippies.

33

HEY, THEY STOLE
OUR IDEA!

MMMBUTTS!
GET IT?!

THEY CAN HAVE IT. OURS IS
THE BOY BAND OF DIGNITY.

WHAT IF EVERYONE
LAUGHS AT US?

RELAX, EVERYONE'S
LAUGHING AT EVERYONE.

BUT IT'S DIFFERENT.
THEY'RE LAUGHING AT
THEIR BUTTS.

THEY'LL BE LAUGHING
AT OUR FACES.

JUST PRETEND YOUR FACE
IS YOUR BUTT!

I'M NOT DOING THIS.
WE'RE GONNA LOOK STUPID.

FINE — GO, THEN.

WE DON'T NEED YOU.

READY?

I GUESS. . . .

You are my fire

The one desire

Believe...

when I say

I WANT IT THAT WAY

CHAPTER 3
Lice Scare

THE SLOG BOYS

Luke
dishes
♥♡♡

3 boys
100 girls!

Little Jim
lawn mower
♥♥♡

Danny
garbage
♥♥♥

These were the only boys in camp. Everyone had a favorite. We were supposed to leave them alone and let them do their jobs in peace, but they always became a point of obsession.

UM . . . I GUESS LUKE.

WHAT?

LUKE IS UGLY.

NO, HE'S NOT! HE'S MYSTERIOUS!

WELL I LIKE DANNY, AND I'M PUTTING A LOVE LETTER FOR HIM IN THE GARBAGE.

I HOPE HE FINDS IT!

WE HEAR THE WHIP-O-WILL . . .

SINGING ABOVE . . .

If you ever expressed any interest in a boy, especially a Slog Boy, the entire camp would burst into song. It happened at least once a day.

ABIGAIL, ABIGAIL

ABIGAIL'S IN LOVE!

WE KNOW HER HEART FLUTTERS

I WISH DANNY WEREN'T SO CUTE.

JUST LIKE A DOVE!

WE'RE GONNA HEAR THIS SONG A BILLION TIMES.

ABIGAIL, ABIGAIL

WELL, WE CAN ALL GO INSANE TOGETHER.

CLINK!

ABIGAIL LOVES DANNY!

42

SMOOCH!

Danny

NOW WE NEED TO DO A CHANT.

CUPID, CUPID, COME TO US!

ALL RIGHT, WHAT TIME IS IT?

2:25.

PERFECT. WE CAN HIDE BEHIND THAT BUSH.

COME ON, Y'ALL. GET DOWN!

45

WHAT IS SHE SO UPSET ABOUT?

DANNY'S LIKE TWENTY YEARS OLD. I'M SURE HE'S NOT INTERESTED IN CAMPERS.

DON'T SQUASH HER FANTASY, SHANNON.

I CAN HEAR YOU. AND I'M NOT SQUASHED.

I'M JUST IRRITATED BECAUSE I'M ALL ITCHY.

ITCHY LIKE . . . SEXUALLY?

UGH, NO, THE NORMAL KIND!

Y'ALL ARE SO IMMATURE!

Evening on the range

LIBBY, TERRIFICO.

MAGGIE . . . UM . . .

CAN YOU GIVE US A MINUTE, LIBBY? GO SHOOT IN THE OTHER STALL.

IT SMELLS LIKE SKUNK OVER THERE.

LIBBY, JUST DO IT.

FINE.

MAGGIE, COME LOOK AT THIS.

I KNOW I'M THE WORST, NICKY.

YEAH, I KNOW YOU KNOW YOU'RE THE WORST. THAT'S **WHY** YOU'RE THE WORST.

I MEAN, GET OUT OF YOUR HEAD. GIVE YOURSELF A FREAKING CHANCE.

TRY THIS. WHEN YOU SHOOT, JUST PRETEND TO BE SOMEONE ELSE.

LIKE WHO?

LIKE ANNIE OAKLEY OR A CIA SNIPER. SOMEONE WHO WOULD NEVER MISS.

Straight through my heart

a single bullet got me

48

BANG

NICE. DO THAT AGAIN.

HEY, THAT'S A ONE-HOLE-GROUP!

BANG

WOW. I GIVE REALLY GOOD ADVICE. I SHOULD WRITE A BOOK.

CALL IT *NICKY'S TRICKIES!*

. . . NO.

KNOCK, KNOCK. I'M HERE TO FETCH MAGGIE. OUR UNIT'S BEING LICE-CHECKED.

NO WAY! MAGGIE CAN'T LEAVE NOW. SHE'S ON FIRE.

I'LL COME RIGHT BACK.

YOU BETTER.

ABIGAIL'S PSYCHOSOMATIC ITCHINESS HAS EVERYONE IN A PANIC.

YOU ARE SO LUCKY THAT REDHEADS NEVER GET LICE.

WHO TOLD YOU THAT?

YOU DID! LAST YEAR!

WOW. I WAS TOTALLY LYING.

LOOKS GOOD. YOU'RE CLEAR.

FELICEITATIONS.

HEH.

SO LONG, SUCKERS.

NEXT.

HEY ERIN.

OH, HEY! SIT ON DOWN.

BY THE WAY, YOU WERE SO GREAT IN THAT BOY BAND THING.

YES. I MEAN... WHAT?

THE BACKSTREET BROTHERS. OR HANSON.

WHICHEVER ONE WAS YOU.

YOU'RE LICE-FREE.

GIVE THIS TO YOUR UNIT HEAD.

LICE ARE CRAAAAZY! GET YOUR HEAD EXAMINED!

camper *Maggie*

inspector *Erin*

WHAT ARE YOU DOING?

NOTHING!

THEN WHY AREN'T YOU ON THE RANGE? I WAS WAITING FOR YOU, GIRL.

SORRY, I FORGOT.

WHAT'S THE MATTER? ARE YOU HAVING AN IDENTITY CRISIS?

WHAT?

WELL, ONE DAY YOU'RE JUST SOME GOOFY LOSER —

EXCUSE ME?

AND THE NEXT DAY YOU'RE SHOOTING ONE-HOLE-GROUPS LIKE A STAR.

BUT MAYBE YOU'D RATHER STAY A LOSER.

LOSERS GET TO CHILL WHILE THE WINNERS DUKE IT OUT.

SO IF YOU'D RATHER **CHILL** THAN BE A WINNER —

NICKY, FINE, I'LL BE A WINNER.

GOOD! GLAD IT'S DECIDED.

HEY, CAN I ASK YOU SOMETHING?

SURE.

HAVE YOU EVER HEARD OF A GAY CODE INVOLVING DOG BREEDS?

WHAT'S A GAY CODE?

YOU KNOW, LIKE A COVERT WAY FOR GAYS TO IDENTIFY EACH OTHER.

INVOLVING DOG BREEDS?

LIKE, MAYBE "COCKER SPANIEL" MEANS GAY, OR "BASSET HOUND" MEANS . . . NOT.

IF I WERE GAY, I'D JUST BARK AT EVERYONE.

DOES THAT ANSWER IT?

. . . I GUESS.

GREAT! THEN I'LL SEE YOU TOMORROW AT THE RANGE.

SLAP

STAY OUTTA YOUR HEAD, MAG.

OK.

I stayed up half the night trying to remember everything I could about her and every interaction we'd ever had.

GRAY!

HUH? WHAT?

I SAID, I HEARD YOU SHOT A ONE-HOLE-GROUP.

YEAH.

WELL CONGRATS. EVERYONE DESERVES TO GET LUCKY ONCE.

THANKS. . . .

The twenty minutes of screaming always ended with a song about sportsmanship and everyone hugging each other.

RIVALS EVER MORE

FRIENDSHIP EVER SURE

HEY! WHY ARE YOU RUNNING?

BECAUSE IT'S FASTER THAN WALKING.

MAG! READY TO BLOW MY MIND?

YES.

LIBBY, CHECK THIS OUT. MAGGIE'S BEEN REBORN.

BUT THAT'S NOT ALL FIVE SHOTS, IS IT?

1, 2, 3, 4, 5.

HUH, NICE JOB.

THANKS.

I used to take full seconds to steady my arm and aim before pulling the trigger. Now I just hoisted the gun and lined up the sights in a single motion, taking the shot the instant my eye glimpsed the center of the bull.

Shooting perfect targets wasn't even the best part. The best part was that while I did it, I didn't have to think about Erin. I could come up for air, and just shoot and shoot and shoot.

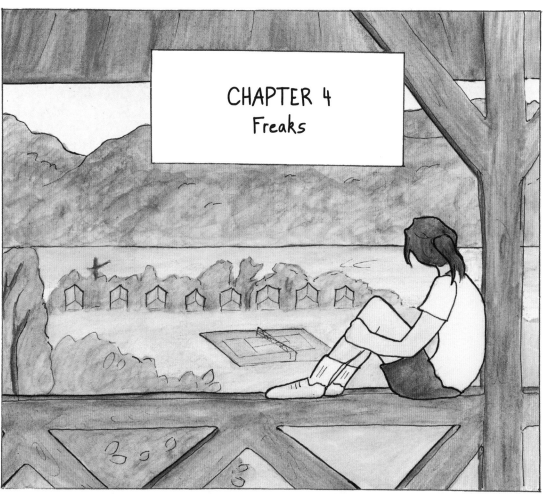

CHAPTER 4
Freaks

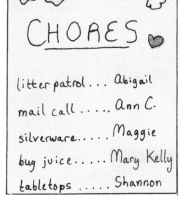

helping hands 😊

CHORES ♡

litter patrol ... Abigail
mail call ..... Ann C.
silverware..... Maggie
bug juice ..... Mary Kelly
tabletops ..... Shannon

SILVERWARE? I THOUGHT I ASKED FOR MAIL CALL.

OH, I SWITCHED YOU!

WHY?

SO YOU COULD BE WITH LUKE!

YOU'RE WELCOME, LOVER GIRL!

JAB

YANK

ERIN. WAIT.

YEAH?

UM, COULD YOU . . . PULL MY HAIR OUT OF MY FACE?

REAL QUICK?

. . . SURE.

DO YOU EVER WEAR A BRAID?

I ALWAYS JUST DO THE SAME THING.

The second she touched me, I wanted to run. I couldn't believe how perverted I was being. You don't trick someone into touching you — not unless you're a creep or a molester.

I could tell I was standing too still and breathing too silently. I prayed she didn't notice, but she must have, she was so close to me.

THERE YA GO.

BYE.

YOU GON' STARE AT THAR SUDS, AIN'T GON' WARSH THEYSEL.

I Recommend...
        by Nicky

    Chapter 1

Being yourself is shit. No one likes you, and that's because of who you are. So be someone else! It's that easy, idiots!

YOU REALIZE YOU'RE ONLY EIGHT BULLS FROM YOUR D.E.? YOU COULD HAVE THIS IN THE BAG, LIKE, TOMORROW.

WE SHOULD SCHEDULE IT. LIKE A C-SECTION.

SUNSET, THE HOUR OF FIRE!

WE COULD SEND INVITATIONS.

OR DUSK! THE HOUR OF SHADOW.

NICKY, WILL YOU SCORE THIS FOR ME?

LIBBY, I DON'T NEED TO SCORE THIS. . . .

YOUR SHOTS ARE ALL OVER THE PLACE. THIS WON'T PASS.

WELL, I'M SORRY IT'S NOT ALL ONE-HOLE-GROUPS LIKE MAGGIE'S. BUT WILL YOU *FUCKING SCORE IT?*

WHOA.

I — I'M SORRY.

I DON'T KNOW WHY I SAID THAT.

HEY, MAGGIE, WHY DON'T YOU . . . GO TAKE A WALK OR SOMETHING?

SOB

ME?

FINE.

SHOVE

. . .

I was supposed to have another two hours of peace from my insane feelings. But now, thanks to Libby, I was being flung out into them. It felt like a tether being snapped. It felt like, if I couldn't shoot, then I had to see Erin immediately or something worse would snap.

I kept thinking about this
pair of girls from two summers
ago, Beth and Ellie. They were
obsessed with horses, in a way the
rest of us had outgrown and found kind
of boring. So we were already used to vaguely
ignoring them.

Then these rumors started going around about
them doing weird things, like wearing each
other's underwear and sneaking out of their
tents at night to go off together. Supposedly
Hailey Ann saw them zipped together in the
same sleeping bag once — completely naked.
I don't know if any of it was true — it
probably wasn't. But they were pretty much
ostracized until the end of camp.

And neither of them ever came back.

This was Wolf Trackers, the nature skills class. It was really unpopular. Usually only one or two girls showed up.

WHATCHA DOIN?

RUB RUB

JUST . . . SCRATCHING MY BACK.

LIKE A BEAR.

BUT WHAT WERE YOU STARING AT?

NOTHING!

LET'S SEE. . . .

BETHANY, DON'T.

It was obvious. That was the worst possible thing she could have said. If it was obvious to Bethany, who I was barely even friends with, then it could be obvious to anyone. So I was doomed.

FREAKS, GOSH, HMM. WHAT MAKES YOU SAY THAT?

COULD IT BE THEIR LOVE OF EQUINES?

OR THE FACT EVERYONE KNEW THEY WERE —

LESBIANS.

WELL, YEAH, THAT . . .

BUT THEY WERE FREAKS TO BEGIN WITH, SO . . .

I MEAN, HORSES OR GIRLS, PICK ONE.

BUT YOU COULD TOTALLY PULL THIS OFF, IF YOU JUST . . . DON'T BE A FREAK!

I'M ALREADY A FREAK.

I'M FOLLOWING HER AROUND LIKE A STALKER.

IT'S ONLY STALKING IF YOUR VIBES ARE BAD. WHAT ARE YOUR VIBES?

HUH?

LIKE, ARE YOU SENDING HER BEAMS OF POSITIVE ENERGY?

. . . NO.

WELL YOU SHOULD! COME ON, LET'S MEDITATE TOGETHER. IT'LL HELP YOU NOT FREAK OUT AS MUCH.

IMAGINE THE SKY IS ON FIRE, THE FIRE OF TRANQUILLITY, AND YOUR MIND IS THE FIRE OF POSITIVITY. AND IT'S PURPLE AND IT'S IN THE SHAPE OF A DOG.

Bethany was clearly bonkers and didn't seem to care that she'd just yanked a huge secret out of me. And whether it stayed a secret wasn't even up to me anymore — it was up to her.

THERE, I FEEL BETTER. YOU?

SURE. NOW LISTEN, YOU CAN'T TELL ANYONE.

THIS IS A SECRET. IT'S NOT, LIKE, A FUN FACT.

FUN FACT: MAGGIE LOVES ER —

BETHANY

AREN'T YOU SUPPOSED TO BE IN RIFLE?

UM, YEAH. BUT I WAS EXILED.

EXILED?!

WE'LL TAKE YOU.

WOLF TRACKERS WELCOMES THE DISPOSSESSED.

COME ON, WE'RE LEARNING FIRE-BUILDING.

I couldn't tell if I was supposed to take her hand or if she was just motioning for me to follow her.

I kept staring at it, trying to decide.

GEEZ, COME ON.

YANK

DID YOU KNOW . . .

THAT . . .

IN 1922, A GIRL DROWNED AT THIS VERY CAMP.

AND SHE WAS SUCH A LONER, IT WAS SIX HOURS BEFORE ANYONE EVEN NOTICED SHE WAS GONE.

SO NOW HER SPIRIT HAUNTS TENT 22, AS PAYBACK FOR HOW EVERYONE IGNORED HER BACK IN THE DAY.

OK . . .

EXCEPT THAT'S NOT A FUN FACT. THAT'S A GHOST STORY.

BUT IT WAS GOOD! I WISH MORE PEOPLE TOLD GHOST STORIES IN THE MIDDLE OF THE DAY.

DING DING DING

Y'ALL GO CLEAN UP FOR DINNER.

I'LL PUT THIS OUT.

HEY MAG, IF YOU GET EXILED AGAIN, COME BACK TO WOLF TRACKERS.

ANYTIME.

THANK YOU! I WILL!

MAYBE I'LL EXILE MYSELF!

EXILE IN THE FOREST. VERY MYTHOLOGICAL.

YES! VERY!

SAY FAREWELL, MAGGIE.

BYE . . .

"ANYTIME." WOW. SHE LOOOOVES YOU.

NO.

NO NO NO. DO NOT EVEN TEASE ME LIKE THAT.

I'M SURE SHE'S NOT, YOU KNOW, GAY.

LIKE YOU'RE QUALIFIED TO SAY.

YOU DIDN'T EVEN KNOW YOU WERE GAY.

I NEVER SAID—

OK, OK, LET'S NOT HAVE A BIG CRISIS.

WHAT DO YOU EVEN CARE IF I HAVE A CRISIS OR NOT?

I THINK YOU'RE JUST WAITING FOR ME TO EMBARRASS MYSELF SO YOU CAN LAUGH YOUR HEAD OFF.

WELL SO WHAT?

AT LEAST SOMEONE WOULD BE LAUGHING.

. . . WHAT DOES THAT MEAN?

YOU KNOW. SMILING? HAR-DEE-HAR?

YOU ARE WAY TOO SERIOUS, MAGGIE THRASH.

YOU CAN'T EVEN PRETEND TO BE A BACKSTREET BOY WITHOUT IT BEING THE MOST SERIOUS THING IN HISTORY.

IT'S CAMP. IT'S SUPPOSED TO BE FUN.

WELL EXCUSE ME FOR NOT HAVING THE TIME OF MY LIFE.

EXCUSE ME FOR HAVING THE SLIGHTEST SENSE OF HUMOR.

COME ON, IT'S FUNNY. YOU LIKE ERIN.

PLUS YOU'RE A MIDGET.

YOUR FACE! YOUR MIDGET RAGE!

HA HA HA HA HA

HEY GUYS. WHAT'S SO HILARIOUS?

JUST . . . HOW SHORT MAGGIE IS.

YUP. LOTTA MILEAGE ON THAT ONE.

WELL, I'LL SCAMPER OFF NOW. SEE YA *ANYTIME.*

I LOOKED FOR YOU AT THE RANGE. NICKY SAID YOU RAN OFF?

I WAS AT WOLF TRACKERS.

SINCE WHEN ARE YOU INTO WOLF TRACKERS?

IT WAS JUST A SPONTANEOUS THING.

At dinner I saw Bethany talking to Erin. I knew she probably wasn't going to blab with a hundred girls around, but I was still so nervous I could barely eat.

BETHANY.

WHAT WERE YOU SAYING TO ERIN?

LISTEN. I THINK WE NEED A CODE FOR WHEN WE NEED TO TALK ABOUT G-A-Y STUFF.

LIKE, "THE BANANA FLIES AT MIDNIGHT."

OK . . .

THE BANANA FLIES AT MIDNIGHT.

COOL!

LET'S MEET SOMEWHERE TONIGHT, AFTER PRAYERS.

LIKE WHERE?

We quickly realized there was nowhere to go.

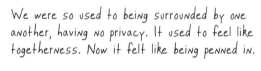

We were so used to being surrounded by one another, having no privacy. It used to feel like togetherness. Now it felt like being penned in.

PLURAL NOUN.

PENISES.

We ended up in the middle of the tennis court with a blanket thrown over our heads.

HIDING IN PLAIN SIGHT.

WE RULE!

SO. HANGIN' WITH MY TINY GAY FRIEND.

OH MY GOD.

I DON'T WANT TO BE A GAY FRIEND. I JUST . . . WISH I WERE A GUY.

A GUY?

YEAH, LIKE A SLOG BOY.

THEN I COULD GIVE HER A FLOWER, OR TAKE HER OUT . . . ON THE BARGE.

EW! ERIN WOULD NEVER GO OUT ON THE BARGE WITH A SLOG BOY.

OR ANY GUY! I'M TELLING YOU, SHE LIKES GIRLS.

BETHANY, I KNOW YOU THINK YOU'RE BEING NICE. BUT PLEASE DON'T —

I'M *NOT* BEING NICE! I CAN PROVE IT. I HAVE EVIDENCE!

YOU DO?

YOU LIKE
GIRLS.

. . . REALLY.

I'M SERIOUS!
IT'S A REAL
QUIZ!

IF YOU LIKE BOYS,
YOU'RE SUPPOSED TO
ANSWER "CIRCLE"
AND "WHITE."

AND YOU LOOK
AT YOUR NAILS
LIKE THIS.

AND YOU LOOK AT
THE SKY LIKE THIS.
WITHOUT RAISING
YOUR CHIN.

BOTH YOU AND
ERIN GOT A ZERO
OUT OF FOUR.

DING

LIKE, IDENTICAL.

UGH, TAPS.

DING

SEE YOU
TOMORROW!

DING

Obviously I didn't think Bethany's quiz results were definitive. But she'd said Erin and I answered every question the same. What were the odds of that?

I decided to ask my brother, who was a math genius. He was in the hospital that summer, getting surgery on his ribs and sternum. He had a sunken chest, which is a genetic deformity where your ribs grow abnormally, caving in around the heart.

They were putting a metal bar in his chest to straighten it out. The timing seemed too bizarre. He was finally going to be normal at the exact time that I wasn't going to be normal anymore.

CHAPTER 6
Predators

HOW DO YOU
DO THIS?

YOU SURE YOU DON'T WANT TO
COME TO THE BLUE RIDGE?

MY PARENTS
WOULD INVITE YOU.

NO THANKS. I
LIKE STAYING HERE.

IT'S PEACEFUL WITH
EVERYONE GONE.

On Sundays all the parents came to visit. Everyone wore Lilly Pulitzer dresses and went to the Blue Ridge Inn in town to have lunch and get manicures. My parents never came because Atlanta was too far away.

BYE, LITTLE ORPHAN! I'LL BRING YOU A CHOCOLATE BAR.

The last barge pulled away, and it was so quiet I could hear a guitar playing across junior camp.

I knew it was her.

I really wanted to stalk her, but with camp so empty, I knew she'd spot me in a second.

It made me realize how much I relied on being one amid a hundred girls — of the flock, concealed by the flock. Now the flock was gone, and without it, I was a single white shirt, standing out against the green tents and green grass.

HI.

97

The counselors' lodge was the most guarded, off-limits place in camp. No campers were ever allowed inside. We weren't even supposed to set foot on the porch.

KNOCK KNOCK

. . . YEAH?

UM, IS NICKY THERE?

NO, IT'S HER DAY OFF.

WHAT ARE YOU DOING HERE?

SORRY, I JUST —

I THINK YOU SHOULD GO BACK TO YOUR TENT.

SLAM

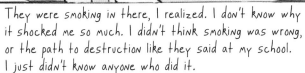

They were smoking in there, I realized. I don't know why it shocked me so much. I didn't think smoking was wrong, or the path to destruction like they said at my school. I just didn't know anyone who did it.

SO DID YOU ENJOY YOUR DAY OF SOLITUDE?

YEAH . . .

PART OF IT, ANYWAY.

PSST! MAG!

I SNEAKED YOU TWO, SO YOU CAN GIVE ONE TO ERIN.

BETHANY, I CAN'T GIVE CANDY TO A COUNSELOR.

I'D PRETTY MUCH BE ASKING TO GET IN TROUBLE.

SHE WOULDN'T GET YOU IN TROUBLE.

OBVIOUSLY.

WHY NOT?

DO YOU HAVE A SUGAR DISPENSATION?

UH . . .

WHATEVER, HAVE YOUR LITTLE SECRET SOCIETY.

IT'S NOT A SOCIETY. IT'S . . .

A BACKSTREET BOYS FAN CLUB.

SNORT

WHACK

AND ERIN'S IN IT?

. . . YEP.

THAT'S SURPRISING. I WOULDN'T HAVE TAKEN HER FOR THE BOY BAND TYPE.

WELL THAT'S EXACTLY THE MAGIC OF BACKSTREET BOYS.

THEY TRANSCEND ALL THAT STUFF.

SHE COULD HAVE **DROWNED**.

I SAVED HER **LIFE**.

♪ WE HEAR THE WHIP-O-WILL SINGING ABOVE

MAGGIE

SLAM

MAGGIE, MAGGIE'S IN LOVE!

OH MY GOD.

IS BETHANY OUTING ME?

AT BREAKFAST?

TO THE WHIP-O-WILL SONG?

. . . JUST LIKE A DOVE! MAGGIE, MAGGIE,

MAGGIE LOVES . . .

MMM?

BETHANY!

CHAPTER 7
Tough Girls

DID YOU HEAR ABOUT HER AND TENNIS BETHANY?

APPARENTLY THEY WERE ON THE TENNIS COURT, BASICALLY NAKED **UNDER A SHEET.**

JESUS, REALLY?

BLYTHE SAID THEY WERE PRETTY MUCH DOING IT WITH **A RACKET.**

THAT IS SO NASTY.

IT'S JUST WHAT HAPPENS WHEN YOU TAKE BOYS AWAY. EVERYONE GOES CRAZY.

APPARENTLY MAGGIE'S OBSESSED WITH VAGINAS AND BETHANY'S OBSESSED WITH TENNIS, SO THEY HAVE, LIKE, AN ARRANGEMENT.

GIRLS.

CAN I SERIOUSLY NOT LEAVE YOU ALONE FOR FIVE MINUTES?

AND WHAT THE HELL HAPPENED TO MAGGIE'S FACE?

UM —

NOTHING.

WE'RE JUST SHOOTING.

Once every summer, we were invaded by boys. It was a tradition with the camp across the river. The boys were usually nice but not that impressive. I always hoped that a moody Kevin Richardson type would manifest amid the sea of khakis and bowl cuts and lacrosse tans, but he never did. And this year, if he did, I doubted I would even care.

WHICH SIDE OF MY FACE LOOKS SEXIER?

UM, THE LEFT.

I TOTALLY AGREE.

LEMME PUT LIPSTICK ON YOU.

YOUR LIPS ARE REALLY CHAPPED, SO YOU NEED A GLOSSY FINISH.

I was used to the way everyone threw themselves on top of each other all the time. Girls held hands and shaved each other's legs and called each other sweetheart. But maybe I wasn't supposed to do that anymore because now everything I did would turn into some gross rumor.

PANTS? YOU'RE WEARING **PANTS?**

CALM DOWN, MARY KELLY. IT'S NOT THE COLLAPSE OF SOCIETY.

I'M GONNA GET SOME HAIR SPRAY. THE TRICK WITH HAIR IS **CONTROLLED DISHEVELMENT.**

HEY.

HEY!

WOW. YOU LOOK CUTE.

THANK YOU!

BUT WHAT HAPPENED TO YOUR FACE?

OH GOD. LIBBY THREW A BOOK AT ME.

SHE'S GOING INSANE BECAUSE I'M BETTER THAN HER.

YEAH, I HEARD YOU'VE BEEN DOMINATING THIS YEAR. . . .

SCOOT OVER.

SO, SHOOTIN' GUNS . . .

IS THAT SOMETHING YOU'RE SERIOUS ABOUT?

I DON'T KNOW IF I'M SERIOUS. . . . NICKY SAYS I COULD GO TO OLYMPIC TRIALS OR SOMETHING. . . .

BUT BETHANY ALWAYS SAYS I'M TOO SERIOUS. SO . . . I GUESS I CAN'T DECIDE WHICH TO BE.

WELL, MAYBE IT'S NOT SOMETHING YOU DECIDE. MAYBE IT'S SOMETHING YOU FEEL.

IF IT FEELS SERIOUS, IT IS SERIOUS.

I BETTER GO.

MY CAMPERS ARE FREAKING OUT.

YOU KNOW, **BOYS.**

BOYS.

SLAM

GULP

CRUSH

HEY.

I HEARD YOU'RE THE TOP SHOOTER AROUND HERE.

UH-HUH.

HOW MANY TARGETS DO YOU HAVE TILL YOU GET D.E.?

TWO.

TWO? YOU GOTTA NAIL THAT BITCH! SEAL THE DEAL!

WELL SHE WAS JUST ABOUT TO BEFORE YOU DICKHEADS INVADED US!

BETHANY!

YOU KNOW I HAVE A DOUBLE D.E. — RIFLE AND SHOTGUN.

I HEARD.

I COULD SHOOT THOSE PESKY TARGETS FOR YOU.

. . . EXCUSE ME?

I'D BE HAPPY TO. JUST TAKE ME TO THE RANGE. IT'LL BE OUR LITTLE SECRET.

WOW, I DON'T NEED SOME DUDE TO CHEAT FOR ME. I'M DOING JUST FINE.

SURE YOU ARE.

WOULD YOU LIKE A DEMONSTRATION?

I WOULD!

YANK

DRAG

HEY NICKY, WILL YOU TAKE US TO THE RANGE?

HUH?

WE WANNA SHOOT.

NOW?!

YEAH, IT'S STILL DAYLIGHT. JUST A FEW TARGETS.

ABSOLUTELY NOT.

WHAT IS WRONG WITH YOU? JUST GO DANCE AND BE **NORMAL.**

SHOVE

SO DO YOU USE AN ARM SLING WHEN YOU SHOOT?

SOMETIMES . . . I SHOOT PRETTY FAST, SO I DON'T USUALLY NEED ONE.

I BET YOU SHOOT REAL FAST.

ROLL

ARE YOU A RIGHT-EYE OR A LEFT-EYE?

RIGHT. I WEAR AN EYEPATCH ON THE LEFT.

SEXY!

YOU THINK SHE'S CUTE?

MAGGIE.

WE SHOULD GET OFF THIS PORCH BEFORE SOMEONE SEES US.

NOT THAT WE CAN'T BE SEEN TOGETHER. . . .

IT'S JUST THAT WE'RE BOTH SO POPULAR . . .

PEOPLE WILL TRY TO TALK TO US

AND I'D RATHER BE ALONE. IF THAT'S OK WITH —

YEAH, LET'S GO.

There's a reason two people sneak out of a dance together. It's to make out. Abigail did it every summer. But I wasn't Abigail, and Erin wasn't some guy, so it was impossible to say whether the standard practices applied. Maybe we were just getting fresh air. Maybe that was an actual thing and not just what people said to disguise what they really wanted.

I THINK YOU WOULD LIKE BOULDER. . . . HAVE YOU EVER LEFT THE SOUTH?

NO . . .

HUH, WHAT IF I KIDNAPPED YOU? WHAT IF I JUST SHOWED UP AT YOUR HOUSE AND DROVE YOU AWAY?

IT WOULD LITERALLY BE A KIDNAPPING. AN ADULT TRANSPORTING A MINOR ACROSS STATE LINES.

IT'S NOT LIKE I'D BE STUFFED IN A TRUNK AND TIED UP WITH A BALL GAG IN MY MOUTH.

JESUS, MAGGIE!

SNAP

IS THAT ABIGAIL?

OH GOD, I BETTER GO BREAK IT UP.

WAIT.

. . . YEAH?

GEE, I'M FLATTERED YOU REMEMBER THAT I EXIST.

HM?

I NEVER SEE YOU ANYMORE. YOU'RE ALWAYS SHOOTING OR HANGING OUT WITH THAT WEIRD TENNIS GIRL.

WHATEVER, FORGET IT.

. . . SORRY.

I'M JUST FEELING A TAD SUICIDAL TODAY.

IF I HEAR THE WHIP-O-WILL SONG ONE MORE TIME I MAY SERIOUSLY END IT ALL.

EVERYONE'S IN LOVE!

EVERYONE'S DEMENTED.

IT'S LIKE, LANDON SETS MY HEART **FREE**, BUT DANNY SETS MY HEART **ON FIRE**.

WHICH IS TRUE LOVE?

I always appreciated Shannon's cynical ways, but now they made me nervous. Would she see any difference between my obsession with Erin and Abigail's obsession with Danny the garbage guy? Probably not.

YOU GAVE ME CAM!

. . . WHAT'S CAM?

CAM. LACEY'S COUSIN. WHO'S AMAZING, BY THE WAY.

OH.

BUT THEN YOU PULL THIS AND MAKE ME FEEL ALL SHITTY AGAIN.

SORRY. BUT IT'S NOT MY JOB TO MAKE YOU FEEL GOOD ABOUT YOURSELF.

YES, IT IS! THAT'S THE EXACT DEFINITION OF FRIENDSHIP!

WE'RE. NOT. FRIENDS.

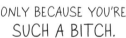

ONLY BECAUSE YOU'RE SUCH A BITCH.

YOU WERE A BITCH WAY BEFORE ME. I WAS JUST RESPONDING.

WELL WE'RE BOTH BITCHES NOW! HAPPY?

GUN SHACK

THIS IS THE ONLY THING IN MY LIFE

AND YOU'RE TAKING IT.

YOU HAVE GREAT HAIR.

SHUT UP.

YOU DON'T GET IT. YOU'RE JUST A KID.

COME ON, YOU'RE LIKE ONE YEAR OLDER THAN ME.

WELL OBVIOUSLY ONE YEAR CAN MAKE A HUGE DIFFERENCE.

BECAUSE IF YOU WERE MORE MATURE, YOU'D GET IT.

I didn't know what it felt like to be mature. I didn't think Libby knew either — the way she cried and whined all the time seemed pretty childish to me. But she was right that I could have been more magnanimous about it. Even now, I didn't really care about her feelings. I mostly cared that she was making me look bad. Maybe if I did something gracious and mature, Erin would hear about it and be impressed. Which I think I realized was possibly the most immature reason to do something nice.

Toward the end of every summer, the senior campers crossed the river to see a play at the community theater in town. The plays tended to be about old-timey values — a fishing hole was often a prominent set piece. But the night wasn't really about the play. It was about the excitement of leaving camp and being in the outside world again. Then, inevitably, you remembered that the outside world is full of old people and hammy theater and that you really weren't missing much.

HI.

HI.

SORRY TO BE ALL COVERT. . . .

I JUST WANTED TO SEE YOU BEFORE YOU LEFT.

COME HERE.

WOW. YOU REALLY ARE SHORT.

HANG ON.

LIFT

THERE.

148

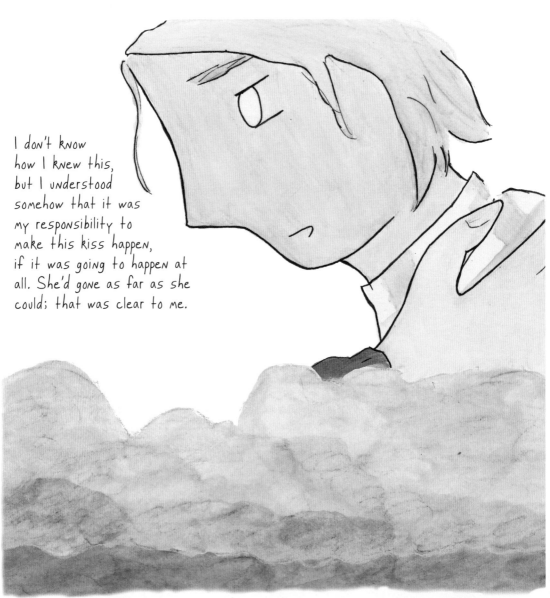

I don't know
how I knew this,
but I understood
somehow that it was
my responsibility to
make this kiss happen,
if it was going to happen at
all. She'd gone as far as she
could; that was clear to me.

IS THAT THUNDER?

It was such a delicate moment,
that's all it took to break it.

150

But I didn't feel confident that I was reading the moment correctly. I mean, I knew, I really knew. But it was too easy to tell myself I was delusional.

Her fingers brushed my neck for a second.

Then she dropped her hand and it was over.

I knew I shouldn't have let Bethany believe that this kiss happened. But in a way, the fact that her lips hadn't touched my lips seemed inconsequential — a dumb technicality. But of course I knew it wasn't dumb. Because until it happened, we both had plausible deniability.

OVER THE RIVER, AND THROUGH THE WOODS

BOX OFFICE

EGLI È IL MAL SORDO QUEL CHE NON VUOLE UDIRE.

NONE SO DEAF AS THOSE WHO CANNOT LISTEN.

WHAT? SAY THAT AGAIN?

The play was about a long-suffering guy who lived with all four of his Italian grandparents. They interfered constantly in his dating life, force-feeding him pasta and wise proverbs.

I wasn't really paying attention. I was thinking about her and swearing to myself that the next time we were alone, I was going to act. It would finally be definitive, one way or the other.

HEY MAG, LOOK.

HM?

HAVE YOU EVER SEEN A HUGER WEDGIE?

LIKE I SAID, GRANDPA . . .

I ALREADY ATE!

SNORT

HA HA HA

COLLECT YOURSELVES OR EXCUSE YOURSELVES. NOW.

HA HA HA HA HA HA

OH MY GOD . . .

HEY, DO YOU HAVE ANY MONEY? WE COULD BUY A SNICKERS.

I BET HE'D GIVE YOU ONE FOR FREE.

WHAT? NO WAY.

WAY! WHEN GIRLS WEAR RED, BOYS' BRAINS EXPLODE.

CONCESSIONS

OK. LET'S GO GET IT, THEN.

WHAT? I WAS KIDDING.

HI.

MAY I HELP YOU?

GOT ANY SWEETS FOR A SWEETIE?

. . . WUT?

I'M SORRY, I JUST — I JUST REALLY NEED A SNICKERS.

SMACK

HA HA HA HA

. . . HERE.

HOLY SHIT

THANK YOU, CONCESSIONS BOY!

CONCESSIONS

I CAN'T BELIEVE THAT WORKED.

HE'S PROBABLY OBSESSED WITH YOU NOW.

HE'LL PROBABLY BE YOUR STALKER.

I DON'T CARE.

I'M NOT SCARED OF BOYS.

SHOULD WE GO BACK IN?

NO. LET'S SEE HOW FAR WE CAN PUSH CONCESSIONS BOY.

YOU SHOULDN'T USE YOUR GIRLISH POWERS FOR EVIL, MAGGIE.

THAT'S NOT WHAT I'M DOING.

YES, IT IS.

157

CAN MAGGIE COME IN MY GROUP?

YOUR TENT'S GOING TO DANNY'S CABIN. IT'S FOURTEENS ONLY.

MAGGIE HAS TO STAY WITH THE FIFTEENS AND SIXTEENS.

THAT'S STUPID. WHY?

UMM . . .

She wouldn't say it, but clearly they wanted to keep the older campers away from the Slog Boys. I found it kind of disturbing, the insinuation that Danny or Luke could see us as WOMEN, as actual objects of desire. That we needed to be separated from them for our own good. I guess it was flattering. . . . But mostly it felt embarrassing and weird.

IT'S ALL RIGHT — MAGGIE CAN GO.

SHE'S FINE.

OMIGOD. IS THAT LIKE A LESBIAN PERK? THAT THEY TRUST YOU AROUND DUDES?

I GUESS. . . .

I. HATE. YOU.

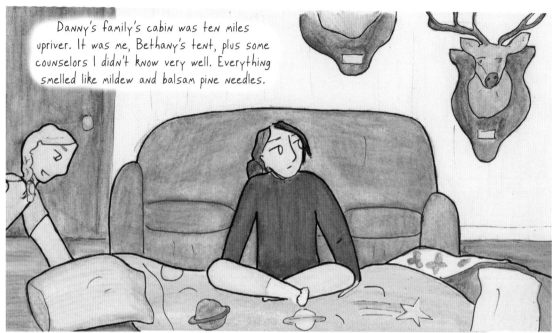

Danny's family's cabin was ten miles upriver. It was me, Bethany's tent, plus some counselors I didn't know very well. Everything smelled like mildew and balsam pine needles.

DANNY, DO YOU HAVE SOMETHING THE GIRLS CAN SLEEP IN?

SURE.

TOSS

WE'RE GONNA SLEEP IN HIS UNDERWEAR?

JUST BE COOL AND PUT IT ON.

Y'ALL.

54 oz

kittle

ARE WE GOING HOME?

I MEAN, BACK TO CAMP?

THE RIVER'S STILL TOO HIGH. WE'RE CHECKING EVERY FOUR HOURS.

SO . . . WHAT ARE WE SUPPOSED TO DO?

I DUNNO. DO WHAT YOU WANT.

4 hours later

EGGS BENEDICT!

4 hours later

4 hours later

AND THE TAMPON WAS IN THERE FOR A **WEEK**.

4 hours later

GAR-DEN
GAR-DEN
GAR-DEN
GAR-DEN
SEC-RET
SEC-RET
SEC-RET
SEC-RET
SEC-RET
SEC-RET
DEN
DEN
DEN

4 hours later

THE GARDEN IS MAGICAL!

4 hours later

4 hours later

RESPECT THE RAIN.

IT'S THE OCEAN REINCARNATED.

4 hours later

EAT IT.

166

Suddenly I really didn't want to be there anymore. It was ridiculous being stuck in this place, away from my gun, and away from Erin. There weren't even that many days of camp left. And here they were, just disappearing. The entire summer was disappearing. And at the end of it, Erin would go back to Colorado and forget about me, all because I never made myself clear.

Dear Erin,
Have you ever met someone where when you're near them it feels like you're going to die

OH MY GOD.

half hour later

KNOCK, KNOCK.

I GOT YOUR STUFF.

WHAT ARE YOU DOING IN HERE?

JUST DOODLING. YOU KNOW . . . **DOODLES.**

BUT NOW I'M DONE.

YOUR FACE WASH LOOKS LIKE JIZ.

THAT IS SO IRONIC.

JIZ FACE, JIZ FACE.

MAGGIE, CAN I TALK TO YOU?

. . . SURE.

SHRUG

CAN Y'ALL CLEAR OUT, PLEASE?

SIT DOWN.

OK . . .

IS SOMETHING WRONG?

I'M NOT TRYING TO SCARE YOU, SWEETHEART.

BUT IT'S MY JOB TO MAKE SURE EVERYONE FEELS SAFE.

I DO FEEL SAFE.

SHE'S NOT, LIKE, PRESSURING ME.

UNFORTUNATELY, YOU'RE NOT MY ONLY CONCERN.

EVERYONE **ELSE** NEEDS TO FEEL SAFE, TOO.

FROM YOU.

PARENTS DON'T SEND THEIR GIRLS HERE TO FROLIC AROUND IN YOUR LESBIAN FANTASY.

I MEAN, WE ALL KNOW ERIN'S . . . THAT WAY.

BUT SHE'S ALWAYS MANAGED TO CONTROL HERSELF.

WE'RE BOTH VERY CONTROLLED.

BELIEVE ME.

YOU BETTER BE. HAVE YOU HEARD OF "DON'T ASK, DON'T TELL"?

. . . YES.

WELL, IT'S THE LAW. AND IT MEANS NO ONE WANTS TO KNOW YOUR BUSINESS.

SO DON'T SHOVE IT IN PEOPLE'S FACES.

IT WASN'T IN YOUR FACE. IT WAS IN THE TRASH.

SWEETHEART, ARE
YOU CRYING?

NO.

DO YOU WANT ME
TO GET BETHANY?

NO.

LISTEN, MAGGIE, YOU'RE GOING
TO BE FINE. JUST DON'T TALK
TO ERIN ANYMORE.

JUST . . . DO WHAT YOU
WERE DOING BEFORE.

What was I doing before? Was I just . . . floating along? Maybe I was better off that way. Because what's ironic is that being in love doesn't actually make you happy. It makes it impossible to be happy. You're carrying this desire now. Maybe if you knew where it came from, you could put it back. But you don't.

CHAPTER 10
The Return of
the Native

DID YOU SEE HIM GET NAKED?

NO. IT WASN'T AN ORGY, ABIGAIL.

I BET IT TOTALLY WAS. YOU SO LUCKED OUT.

I WAS AT MARY ASHTON'S HOUSE.

HER MOM MADE US FOLD CHURCH LEAFLETS.

WE ATE CREAMED CORN.

HEY LESBIAN.

WHIRL

TRIP

LESLIE ANN. LESLIE ANN!

UGH.

MY KNEE.

YOU CRUSHED ME.

SORRY, LEXI.

If you ever got injured at camp, you were pretty much screwed. The nurse was an ancient old lady who believed the solution for everything was a vinegar soak. One summer a girl fell off her horse, and it was 20 hours before anyone called the hospital, even though she was screaming in pain and it turned out she'd broken her collarbone.

BOO-BOO SHACK

JUS' KEEP YA WEIGHT OWF IT, SUGAH. IT'LL RIGHT ITSELF IN NO TIME.

THAT LOOKS HORRIBLE.

WILL YOU HELP ME GET TO ARCHERY?

OW.

OW.

Maybe she hadn't seen me, or maybe she was busy. I didn't necessarily need to panic just because she didn't say hi, or even wave.

PEOPLE WHO ARE BETTER DESERVE TO WIN, MAGGIE.

IT'S CALLED A MERITOCRACY. IT'S THE FAIREST SYSTEM ON EARTH.

STOP PEER-PRESSURING ME, NICKY.

I'M NOT YOUR PEER.

I'M OLDER AND WISER, AND I'M TELLING YOU TO SHOOT A DAMN TARGET.

I'LL BE RIGHT BACK.

HI.

I'd planned to regale her with comical tales from my 82 hours at Danny's family's cabin, presuming she would at least acknowledge that I'd been gone. But she didn't.

UM, DID TAMMY SAY SOMETHING TO YOU?

BECAUSE SHE —

MAGGIE, IT'S NOT A GREAT TIME.

SORRY.

AND . . . I MEAN THAT IN A LARGER SENSE.

LIKE, HOW YOU KNOW IF SOMETHING'S IN THE STARS.

OR NOT.

WELL . . . YOU'RE THE ASTRONOMY MAJOR.

YEAH.

I AM.

ANYWAY . . . SEE YA.

SEE YA . . .

RAKE

RUMMAGE

I don't know why it occurred to me to do this. Maybe I saw it in a movie. I think the girl in *Legends of the Fall* does it right before she kills herself.

But I wasn't thinking of that at the time. I wasn't thinking of anything. It's just this mythological desire you have to suddenly — to be unrecognizable to yourself.

OH MY GOD.

NOT BAD!

BE CAREFUL, OR ELSE IT WILL FLOP INTO A BOWL CUT.

MUSS IT UP EVERY NOW AND THEN.

LIKE THIS?

YEAH.

SO . . . I BASICALLY JUST SAVED YOUR LIFE.

MY FEE IS THAT YOU HAVE TO TELL ME WHY YOU'VE BEEN SUCH A WEIRDO LATELY.

I REALLY DON'T WANT TO.

YOU **HAVE** TO.

OR WE'RE NOT FRIENDS ANYMORE.

I'M SERIOUS.

ARE YOU GAY? THAT'S WHAT EVERYONE'S SAYING.

EVERYONE? WHO'S EVERYONE?

OH, JUST THOSE BITCHY SIXTEENS. NO ONE'S PAYING ATTENTION.

EXCEPT NOW THEY MIGHT. THIS HAIRCUT IS **QUITE** GAY.

OH, MY GOD. WHY DID I DO THIS?

NOT TO JUDGE YOUR PREDILECTIONS, BUT **BETHANY**?

SHE'S SO ANNOYING.

IT'S NOT BETHANY.

. . . IS IT ME?

ROLL

JUST CHECKING.

UGH.

UGH. POOR YOU.

YOU KNOW . . . YOU COULD HAVE TOLD ME.

I'M NOT LIKE EVERYONE ELSE HERE.

I THOUGHT YOU KNEW THAT.

I DO. I JUST . . .

I WAS AFRAID YOU WOULD THINK IT WAS LAME.

WHAT? BEING INTO CHICKS?

NO, JUST . . . BEING INTO ANYONE.

189

I had no idea where I was, or where camp was. Usually when this happened, Mary Kelly or someone was right behind me. Usually I tripped over things and woke everyone up.

But this time . . . there was no one. It was creepy. It was like I was becoming this secretive and stealthy person, even in my sleep. And now I had to wait for the sun to come up to find my way back.

CHAPTER 11
One More Day

BOYS, AIR-CONDITIONING, EVERYTHING NOT SMELLING LIKE MILDEW. NO FREAKING CRICKET SOUNDS, MY DOGS, CHEERLEADING, *BUFFY*, MY CAR, NACHOS, WEARING WHAT I WANT, LIPSTICK, SLEEPING IN, MY BOYFRIEND LIKE, EVERY EPISODE OF *DAWSON'S CREEK*, DIET COKE, PEDICURES, MANI

You knew camp was almost over when everyone started talking about all the stuff they couldn't wait to do when they got home. And the daily schedule of things started to fall apart. Counselors stopped caring whether you showered at the appointed hour or skipped prayers or wore open-toed shoes. All those rigid rules seemed suddenly dumb, and you'd hear everyone saying, "What are they gonna do, send us home?"

MAGGIE.

I NEED TO TALK TO YOU. NOW.

OKAAAAY . . . HANG ON, LEXI.

WHAT HAVE YOU DONE TO YOURSELF?

SHRUG

ARE YOU HAVING A NERVOUS BREAKDOWN?

SHRUG

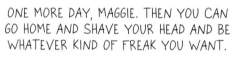

ONE MORE DAY, MAGGIE. THEN YOU CAN GO HOME AND SHAVE YOUR HEAD AND BE WHATEVER KIND OF FREAK YOU WANT.

TILL THEN I NEED YOU TO KEEP IT TOGETHER, OK?

. . . OK.

AND IF YOU'RE GOOD, I HAVE SOMETHING REALLY SPECIAL PLANNED.

WINK

IF I'M **GOOD**? WHAT DOES THAT MEAN?

. . . YOU KNOW WHAT IT MEANS.

WHOA.

NICE HAIR.

YOU LOOK LIKE A LITTLE BOY OFF TO SHOOT A SQUIRREL FOR DINNER.

. . . YOU GONNA SHOOT AN ACTUAL TARGET TODAY?

NO.

I TOLD YOU, I'M WAITING FOR LIBBY.

COME **ON**!

LIBBY'S NOT GONNA MAKE IT. SHE'S WOUND UP SO TIGHT SHE COULDN'T SHOOT HER OWN FOOT.

DO YOU REALLY WANT TO GO HOME WITH **ONE** TARGET LEFT?

AT LEAST SHOOT SOME PRACTICE BULLS. YOU DON'T HAVE TO SHOOT THE WHOLE THING. JUST TAKE A FEW SHOTS.

UGH, NICKY, FINE!

YES!

CLAP

OK, JUST SHOOT WHERE I TELL YOU. IT'LL BE LIKE A GAME!

ATTENTION Y'ALL. MAGGIE THRASH JUST SHOT HER D.E.!

I THINK YOU'RE THE FIRST PERSON IN HISTORY TO **ACCIDENTALLY** SHOOT THEIR DISTINGUISHED EXPERT.

WHY ARE YOU ALWAYS IN MY FACE?

YOU DON'T EVEN TAKE RIFLE!

JESUS, DON'T SAY THAT WITH GUNS AROUND!

WHAT'S GOING ON DOWN THERE?

COME ON, LET'S JUST GO.

CONGRATULATIONS ON BEING A DISTINGUISHED **ASSHOLE**!

AT LEAST I'M NOT A DISTINGUISHED **TWAT**.

SNORT

DISTINGUISHED TWAT?

HA HA HA

HA HA HA

OH MY GOD, WHAT IS THAT GIRL'S PROBLEM?

SHE'S SUCH A VIOLENT FREAK.

THAT'S THE SECOND TIME SHE'S ATTACKED ME.

AND IT'S ALWAYS, LIKE, ON LIBBY'S BEHALF.

I WISH I HAD SUCH A WEIRDLY DEVOTED FRIEND.

I'M TOTALLY WEIRDLY DEVOTED.

PUNCH

IT JUST SHOWS IN A DIFFERENT WAY.

I MEAN, DO YOU REALLY NEED ME TO GO AROUND ATTACKING YOUR RIVALS?

NO.

EXACTLY. YOU JUST NEED SOMEONE TO CHILL WITH.

TO BE REAL WITH.

I HEARD SHE'S BEEN CRYING ALL DAY.

ARE YOU GONNA APOLOGIZE TO HER?

NO. IT WAS AN ACCIDENT. NICKY TRICKED ME.

YOU REALIZE NO ONE BELIEVES THAT. . . .

SHRUG

HEY, WHAT DID ERIN THINK OF YOUR HAIR?

I DON'T KNOW. . . .

SHE'S BEEN AVOIDING ME.

WHADDA THEY GONNA DO? SEND ME HOME?!

HA HA HA

Shanna

WELL, TONIGHT'S YOUR LAST CHANCE.

I HEARD SHE'S NOT COMING BACK NEXT YEAR.

HEARD FROM WHO?

I DUNNO. SOME JUNIORS.

I MEAN, SHE'S PRETTY OLD FOR THIS PLACE.

ATTENTION, LADIES. THERE ARE CANDLES HERE FOR EVERYONE.

CANDLES   CANDLES

The turn of the millennium was the height of "everyone's a winner" parenting. Most camps were dispensing with awards or else making sure everyone got one, so no one would feel left out or have low self-esteem. Not so with us; here we did things the old way. There were only a few awards, and only a few girls got them, and everyone else envied them bitterly.

For a second I actually felt optimistic. I mean, I **really** didn't want to go home. What was I going to do — tell my parents I liked girls now? I was supposed to be doing my pre-debutante cotillion that fall, and there was zero room to be gay in that crowd. But maybe if I got Spirit of Rifle, it would be a little better. . . . My dad loved guns. He had a whole closet full of them for bird hunting. And my mom loved displaying fancy things. Maybe that would be enough to distract them.

Friendliest Camper

Happiest Camper

Senior Camp Achievement

LOOK AT JENNY'S FACE.

SHE TOTALLY THOUGHT SHE WAS GETTING HAPPIEST CAMPER.

NOT SO HAPPY NOW. . . .

THIS NEXT AWARD GOES TO A GIRL WHO'S HAD SOME UPS AND DOWNS THIS SUMMER.

THIS SHOULD BE A PRETTY BIG **UP**.

I hoped Erin was watching. Because once I got that silver cup, I wouldn't just be some barely-fifteen-year-old camper she randomly met. I'd be the Spirit of Rifle, and then no one could shame her for liking me.

SPIRIT OF RIFLE IS
LIBBY MULLIGAN.

WOW, THAT'S A CRIME.

I don't know why I was so mad. It hadn't even occurred to me that I could get Spirit of Rifle before Bethany mentioned it. But it was amazing how quickly I'd come to see that award as **mine.** And amazing how quickly it was taken away.

NOW FOR OUR SPECIAL AWARD. THE ONE WE GIVE TO THE GIRL WHO EMBODIED OUR SPECIAL SPIRIT.

I kept expecting someone to tell me to sit down. Maybe Shannon had misheard my name or was messing with me. But the Honor Girls of summers past were just staring at me with their creepy, affectionate smiles. They were the prettiest, nicest girls in camp. The kind who went around comforting homesick juniors and organizing sing-alongs. I had no idea what I was doing with them.

Then I realized . . . It was my reward for keeping quiet about my freakish feelings. Which had less to do with honor and more to do with being a huge coward.

Maybe I should have felt victorious, but instead I just felt embarrassed and kind of appalled — that a sham this big was on **me**.

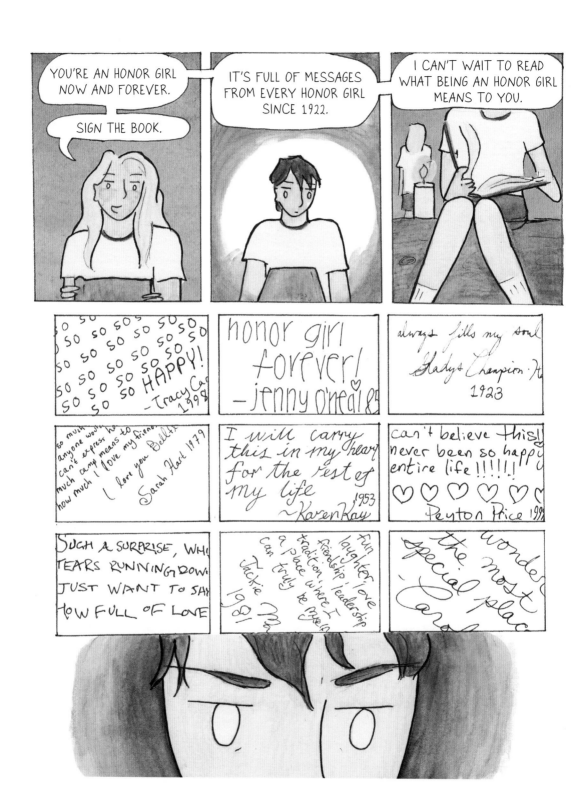

This is the Book of Frauds because I shouldn't even be here and everyone is so fake it makes me want to go on a killing spree.
HONOR GIRL IS THE STUPIDEST FUCKING THING I'VE EVER HEARD

OH MY GOD.

On my gosh I never thought this day would come I love this place so much now ♡ fills my ♡ ♡

I don't know what to say because I didn't expect to be part of this camp history forever. I don't feel great about this. I feel really weird. But I'm gonna sign this book now. I guess if you're reading this it means you're Honor Girl too, so congrats. I hope it means something?
                                            —Maggie Thrash, 2000
P.S. I just realized I'm the first Honor Girl of the entire millennium. Jesus Christ, this camp will probably outlast us all.

... I WISH I COULD TELL YOU THAT ...

I THINK YOU'RE WONDERFUL

BUT SOMETHING STOPS ME AND NERVOUSLY I FLEE ...

WHILE THE MEMORY OF YOUR FACE ... IT BURNS IN MY MIND.

IT **BURNS** HER MIND, MAGGIE!

SHAKE

YOU ARE MY UNTOUCHABLE ANGEL

BUT COURAGE TAKES ITS TIME ...

OH. MY. GOD. WHAT ARE YOU GONNA DO?

DO?

YOU HAVE TO, LIKE, **GO** TO HER!

GO TO HER, THRASH!

I'M NOT GONNA "GO TO HER" WITH FIVE BILLION CHILDREN AROUND.

THE SONG'S PROBABLY NOT EVEN ABOUT ME.

IT'S PROBABLY ABOUT . . . A DOG.

A **DOG**? AN UNTOUCHABLE **DOG**?

YEAH, LIKE, IT ROLLED AROUND IN GARBAGE, SO IT'S ALL FILTHY.

ARE YOU SERIOUS?

MAGGIE, YOU'RE LETTING THIS MOMENT DISAPPEAR.

IT'S DISAPPEARING AS WE SPEAK!

THEN JUST LET IT, BETHANY!

NOT EVERY MOMENT HAS TO HAPPEN.

CHAPTER 12
Good-byes

Our good-byes were never very heartfelt. The last morning was so aggravating — trying to get your stuff together, other people's parents everywhere — you didn't feel like crying or getting emotional about it. I was always one of the last to leave, since my mom had farther to drive. The counselors would start taking down tents, like they couldn't even wait till we were gone.

I hope you are having a fun summer while I languish in this sanatorium for the deformed. Despite the acute and ongoing pain of having my sternum LITERALLY RECONSTRUCTED, I definitely definitely care about your problems, i.e., emerging gynephilia. Just kidding, I don't. But if I did, I would say that given the scenario you proposed, the odds are very low:

$$\frac{4^2}{(2^2 \times 2^2 \times 2^2 \times 2^2) - 4^2} \quad = \quad \frac{16}{240} \quad = \quad \frac{1}{15}$$

However, you neglected to specify whether lower odds correlate to a higher degree of innate/manifest Sapphism or the inverse. So I am unable to draw a firm conclusion. Additionally I fail to see how this proposition relates in any way to sexual preferences.

bye
Drew

WHATCHA READIN'?

HEY!

IT'S FROM MY BROTHER.

I JUST GOT IT TWO SECONDS AGO.

HEY, CONGRATS ON HONOR GIRL.

THANKS . . .

I DON'T REALLY KNOW WHY I GOT IT . . .

I DO.

. . .

BECAUSE YOU WERE SO GREAT WITH LEXI WHEN SHE SPRAINED HER KNEE, HELPING HER GET AROUND AND STUFF.

OH . . .

I THINK THAT'S MY MOM.

LISTEN, I HAVE TO GO DO SOMETHING.

RIGHT NOW?

FIGHTING BISHOP INN,
KNOXVILLE, TN

KNOCK
KNOCK

YOU'RE NOT
WEARING **THAT**?
WHAT ABOUT YOUR
LILLY PULITZER?

UM, THAT'S NOT
REALLY MY STYLE
ANYMORE. . . .

OF COURSE IT IS!
LILLY PULITZER IS
THE VERY ESSENCE
OF STYLE.

TOSS

Brigadoon is a musical about an enchanted village in Scotland that appears once every 100 years.

Then one day an American tourist stumbles upon it.

He falls in love with a bonnie lassie and decides to stay in Brigadoon forever.

But he can't because the enchantment breaks and Brigadoon disappears into the mist.

THIS WASN'T ON THE MAP. . . .

FIONA! FIONA!

CHAPTER 13
Civilization

MONTHS LATER, IN ATLANTA

I didn't bother telling my parents. It's not like I had an actual girlfriend or any immediate reason to upset the family universe. Except I was so depressed, I hadn't done any homework or taken a shower in a month.

When my mom finally noticed, she said she refused to be seen with me in public until I washed my hair. Which was fine with me because I didn't feel like going to church or pre-debutante cotillion luncheons or the mall anyway. My mom got pretty good at making excuses.

Both times I tried telling someone that I was possibly gay now, it ended with them insisting to me that I wasn't. The first was my best friend since 6th grade. The second was my gym teacher.

It was basically the same speech she gave to girls who tried to get out of sit-ups because they were on their periods.

I sent Erin three letters addressed to the University of Colorado.

I didn't know if she never got them or just never replied.

After a few months I gave up wondering either way.

I spent most of that year in the basement with my brother watching *Babylon 5*. I got really obsessed with it, partly because of this maddening hint that Lieutenant Ivanova was a lesbian.

When no one was around, I'd sit on the roof of the house and shoot acorns with my dad's .22. You could do that sort of thing in Georgia without anyone calling the police.

It wasn't about staying sharp. It was about feeling that feeling again — aim, fire, unload — of being totally focused yet totally blank. And the ringing in your ears that stayed with you long after you pulled the trigger.

I shouldn't have gone back the next summer, but I did. If there was the slightest chance that she would be there, I had to be there too.

She wasn't.

Everything was the same. That shouldn't have surprised me — wasn't it always the same? But it seemed unbelievable this time that things could just go on, oblivious of me, with no sympathy for the fact that I was a different person now.

It turns out that once you have your D.E., there's not much left to do. I started shooting random stuff, but after a while, that started to feel pointless. What was the point of being that good? It's not like I was a hunter or an assassin.

I was just a girl with a weirdly deadly toy.

WHERE DID HE GET THAT GIANT LOLLIPOP?

IS THERE A CARNIVAL NEARBY?

OH, YOU CAN GET THOSE AT WALMART NOWADAYS.

REALLY? I'VE NEVER BEEN TO WALMART.

WHAT?

SHRUG

MY MOM SAYS WALMART IS TRASHY.

WELL, YEAH, IT'S TOTALLY TRASHY.

AND I'M TOTALLY TAKING YOU THERE.

COME ON.

WAIT, NOW?

SURE, THIS PLACE ISN'T GOING ANYWHERE.

IT'S BEEN HERE A THOUSAND YEARS.

It was hard to know what to talk about. What had we talked about at camp? I couldn't even remember. Obviously not my SAT scores. At camp no one talked about stuff like that, like we'd all unconsciously agreed to leave those things behind.

And now, instinctively I guess, Erin and I were doing the opposite. Leaving camp behind, not talking about it, maybe so it would feel less foreign and weird to be stranded outside it.

LOOK, THEY HAVE EVERY KIND OF SODA.

EVERYDAY $ VALUES

NO, YOU GOTTA GET THE BIG CUP. THE 60-OUNCE.

MAKE IT A SUICIDE.

GULP

WHOA. IT'S HEAVY!

I WANNA SEE YOU DRINK THE WHOLE THING.

WHAT? THAT'S NOT A SUICIDE, THAT'S AN AMICICIDE.

WHAT DOES THAT MEAN?

AMICICIDE. IT'S, UM, THE KILLING OF A FRIEND.

. . . DID YOU GET MY LETTERS?

LETTERS? NO.

DO YOU NOT BELIEVE ME?

SHRUG

I THOUGHT ABOUT YOU. A LOT.

ACTUALLY I WROTE A SONG ABOUT YOU A FEW MONTHS AGO. . . .

A few months ago? "Untouchable Angel" was two years ago. Maybe Bethany was wrong that it was about me.

WHAT'S IT CALLED?

WAIT. NEVER MIND, DON'T TELL ME. IT'LL MAKE ME FEEL SELF-CONSCIOUS.

OH, DON'T WORRY. THE TITLE IS VERY VAGUE AND REVEALS NOTHING.

"BROWN HAIR PERSON FEELINGS MELODY."

ARE YOU OK?

YOU SEEM . . . TIGHTLY WOUND.

GAHH!

WHOA.

OH MY GOD.

SORRY.

I'M JUST . . . I'M TRYING TO ACT NORMAL, BUT I'M A TAD . . . OVERWHELMED.

IT'S OK . . . WALMART CAN HAVE THAT EFFECT.

SO CAN A THOUSAND GRAMS OF SUGAR.

HOW LONG WAS THE DRIVE HERE FROM BOULDER?

NOT BAD. SEVEN HOURS.

SEVEN HOURS?

MAYBE THAT SEEMS FAR TO YOU. . . . OUT HERE, EVERYTHING'S FAR APART.

WHOA. YOU STILL HAVE THIS?

YEAH . . . BUT IT'S FALLING APART.

. . . I MEAN, STARS ARE PRETTY, YEAH, BUT WHAT DO THEY **DO**? WHAT DO THEY **MEAN**? WITHOUT MATH THEY'RE JUST . . . FARAWAY SPARKLY THINGS THAT SHOW UP AT NIGHT.

I'M TERRIBLE AT MATH. I GUESS I'LL NEVER KNOW WHAT THE STARS MEAN.

WELL, I'M EXCELLENT AT MATH, SO . . .

I CAN JUST TELL YOU.

She was going to kiss me. That was clear. I couldn't delude myself this time. I didn't even want to delude myself. I was older now, and I'd spent the last two years hoping a moment exactly like this would happen.

Except the room felt overly warm. It felt like my hands were going numb and I couldn't quite see her properly.

Something had changed. She was wary of me now, I could tell. Like she'd realized I wasn't as mature or self-possessed as I'd seemed. That this was way too big of a deal to me. She was smiling, but in a big-sisterly way that made me wish I'd stayed unconscious.

IT WAS GREAT TO SEE YOU, MAGGIE. I ALWAYS FELT TERRIBLE THAT WE NEVER SAID GOOD-BYE.

YOU KNOW . . . THAT LAST DAY.

It seemed weird that she said "we." As if it had been a fluke or a mutual error.

I didn't say anything. Why did it always feel like this love was up to me?

COME HERE.

It wasn't a good hug. Our arms sort of knocked together, and then she pulled away from me. She didn't even take off her seat belt.

DOUBLE WHISKEY?

SURE.

HA. TRY A SHIRLEY TEMPLE.

SWING

I thought that if I waited, she would come back. She had to come back. It couldn't be this stupid twice.

it's over, it's

266

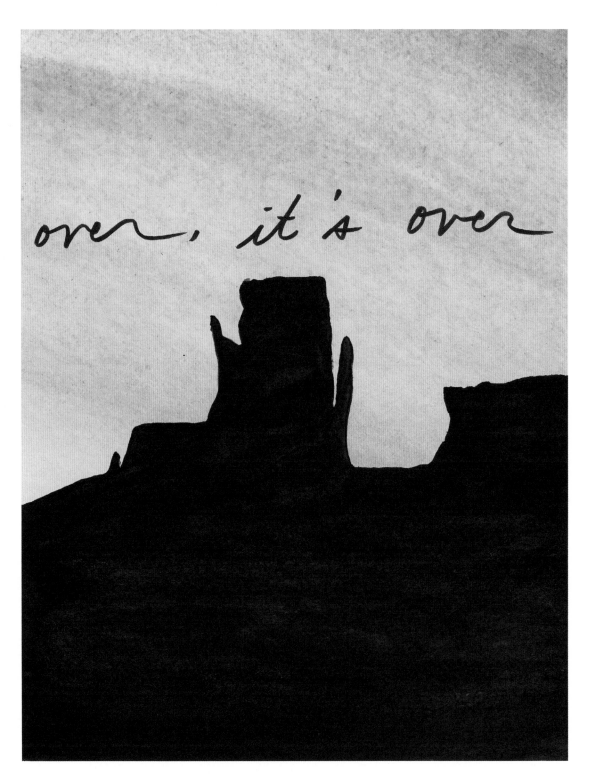

This is a work of nonfiction. The events and experiences detailed herein have been described from the author's memory. Some names, identities, and circumstances have been changed to protect the privacy and/or anonymity of the various individuals involved.

———————

Maggie Thrash attended Hampshire College and the Sewanee University of the South. She hasn't shot a gun in ten years.

———————

All my gratitude to Stephen Barr, whose idea this was.

Thank you to the universal mind at Candlewick, particularly my editor Katie Cunningham, Liz Bicknell, Laila Milevski, Sherry Fatla, and Gregg Hammerquist.

Special thanks to my BFF Nico. I'm pretty sure everyone thinks he's imaginary, but he's real and I couldn't have made this without him.

Copyright Acknowledgments

To Ms. Phillipoff, as promised

First paperback edition 2016

Library of Congress Catalog Card Number 2014951805
ISBN 978-0-7636-7382-6 (hardcover)
ISBN 978-0-7636-8755-7 (paperback)

22 23 24 25 CCP 10 9 8 7 6

Printed in Shenzhen, Guangdong, China

This book was typeset in Maggie Thrash.
The illustrations were done in watercolor pencil
and pen, and completed digitally.

Candlewick Press
99 Dover Street
Somerville, Massachusetts 02144

visit us at www.candlewick.com